W9-CVN-578

The

FIRST FIVE YEARS

A Child's Record Book and Keepsake

Caroline Ash

DK PUBLISHING, INC.

A DK Publishing Book

Design Bernard Higton

Editor Lorraine Turner
Senior Managing Editor Krystyna Mayer
Deputy Art Director Carole Ash
DTP Designer Bridget Roseberry
Production Sarah Coltman

Photography
Dorling Kindersley would like to thank the following for
the photographs appearing in the book:
Paul Bricknell, Martin Brigdale, Jan Burton, Steve Gorton, David Johnson,
Dave King, David Murray, Stephen Oliver, Tim Ridley, Guy Ryecart,
Jules Selmes, Steve Shott, Colin Walton, and Alex Wilson

First American edition, 1998
2 4 6 8 10 9 7 5 3 1

Published in the United States by DK Publishing, Inc.
95 Madison Avenue, New York, New York 10016

Visit us on the World Wide Web at http://www.dk.com

ISBN 0–7894–3514–4

Reproduced in Italy by Colorlito Rigogliosi S.R.L., Milan
Printed and bound in Singapore by Tien Wah Press

CONTENTS

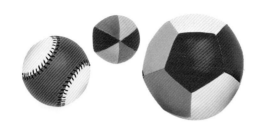

The Birth 4
The Naming Ceremony 6
The Family Tree 7

THE SECOND YEAR

Memorable Milestones 17 ◆ Personality 18
Favorite Things 19 ◆ Daily Life 20
Bath Time and Water Play 21
Vacations and Outings 22
Holidays at Two 24 ◆ Second Birthday 25

THE FOURTH YEAR

Memorable Milestones 37 ◆ Personality 38
Favorite Things 39 ◆ Daily Life 40
Vacations and Outings 41
Holidays at Four 42 ◆ Fourth Birthday 43

THE FIRST YEAR

Memorable Milestones 9 ◆ Personality 10
Favorite Things 11 ◆ Daily Life 12
Vacations and Outings 13
Holidays at One 14 ◆ First Birthday 15

THE THIRD YEAR

Memorable Milestones 27 ◆ Personality 28
Favorite Things 29 ◆ Daily Life 30
Nursery School 31 ◆ Vacations and Outings 32
Holidays at Three 34 ◆ Third Birthday 35

THE FIFTH YEAR

Memorable Milestones 45 ◆ Personality 46
Favorite Things 47
Daily Life 48 ◆ First Days at School 49
Vacations and Outings 50
Holidays at Five 52 ◆ Fifth Birthday 53

Growth Record 54 ◆ Medical Record 56

THE BIRTH

May 16, 2019 8:29 am
DATE AND TIME

Blanchard Valley Hospital Findlay, ohio
PLACE

5 lbs 2oz. 18.5 inches
WEIGHT AND LENGTH

COLOR OF EYES

COLOR OF HAIR

Brown

Daddy
BABY LOOKS LIKE . . .

COMMENTS ON THE BIRTH

HOSPITAL BRACELET

BIRTH ANNOUNCEMENT

SPECIAL MESSAGES FROM FAMILY AND FRIENDS

YOUR BABY'S FIRST
PHOTOGRAPH

Grandma + great-grandma

VISITORS AND GIFTS

ZODIAC SIGN

CHINESE BIRTH SIGN

BIRTHSTONE

ZODIAC FLOWER

THE NAMING CEREMONY

Blake Anthony Kessler

YOUR BABY'S FULL NAME

GUESTS PRESENT

REASON FOR THE CHOICE OF NAME

DATE AND TIME OF CEREMONY

LOCATION OF CEREMONY

YOUR BABY'S OUTFIT

DESCRIPTION OF CEREMONY

GIFTS RECEIVED / FROM WHOM

GRANDMOTHER
PHOTOGRAPH

GRANDFATHER
PHOTOGRAPH

GRANDMOTHER
PHOTOGRAPH

GRANDFATHER
PHOTOGRAPH

THE FAMILY TREE

MOTHER
PHOTOGRAPH

FATHER
PHOTOGRAPH

BROTHERS AND SISTERS
PHOTOGRAPH

BABY
PHOTOGRAPH

BROTHERS AND SISTERS
PHOTOGRAPH

THE FIRST YEAR

URING THE FIRST FEW WEEKS of life your baby has to adjust to surviving outside the womb. At this time his needs are very basic: he eats, cries, and sleeps for much of the time. As your baby matures, he begins to develop an interest in the surrounding world, to react to different stimuli, and to want to explore his immediate environment.

Your baby learns through his senses and by using his body. Anything that is not within his range of vision, smell, or touch does not exist for him. He will discover his body by moving his limbs constantly, kicking his legs rhythmically and waving his arms around. A very young baby is limited in his ability to communicate his feelings, and initially can only cry when distressed. In the course of his first year, however, your baby begins to make a wide variety of cooing and babbling sounds, and toward the end of the year may articulate the beginning of an identifiable word. At this stage of life a baby's parent or principal caregiver is the center of his world, and he relies on her constant presence for his well being. He can easily recognize her face and is comforted by her voice.

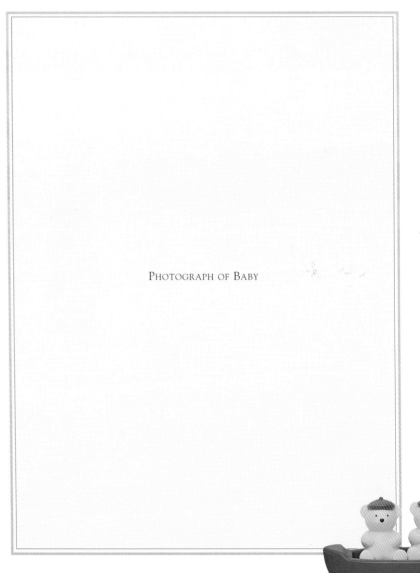

PHOTOGRAPH OF BABY

MEMORABLE MILESTONES

FIRST SMILES

FIRST HOLDS HEAD UP

Aug.   2019

FIRST HOLDS OBJECT IN HANDS

Dec. 8, 2019

GROWS FIRST TOOTH

Dec. 8, 2019

FIRST PICKS UP OBJECT WITH FINGER AND THUMB

July 29, 2019

FIRST SLEEPS THROUGH THE NIGHT

May 2020

FIRST EATS UNAIDED

Oct. 2019

FIRST TURNS OVER

January 2020

FIRST SITS UP UNAIDED

FIRST CRAWLS

FIRST STANDS UNAIDED

Dec. 2020

TAKES FIRST STEPS

SAYS FIRST WORD

FIRST USES A WORD FOR FATHER OR MOTHER

TREASURED MOMENTS

PERSONALITY

THINGS THAT MAKE YOUR BABY . . .

SMILE OR LAUGH

CALM AND SETTLED

EXCITED

BECOME UPSET

PHOTOGRAPH

SLEEP PATTERNS

SPECIAL TRAITS

FAVORITE THINGS

FOOD

DRINK

CUDDLY TOYS

BATH TOYS

OTHER TOYS

ANIMALS

PHOTOGRAPH OF BEST FRIEND

SONGS AND LULLABIES

FAVORITE ADULTS

SPECIAL FRIENDS

DAILY LIFE

MORNING

FEEDING SCHEDULE

MIDDAY

FAVORITE TIME OF DAY

AFTERNOON

WORST TIME OF DAY

BATH TIME

SPECIAL MOMENTS

BEDTIME

VACATIONS AND OUTINGS

FIRST VACATION

DATE *June*

PLACE

THE TRIP

WHERE YOU STAYED

YOUR BABY'S BEHAVIOR

AMUSING INCIDENTS

SPECIAL MEMORIES

VACATION PHOTOGRAPH

MEMORABLE OUTINGS

VISITS TO RELATIVES AND FRIENDS

OTHER OUTINGS

HOLIDAYS AT ONE

WHERE HOLIDAY WAS SPENT

THE HOLIDAY MEAL

PHOTOGRAPH

WHO WAS THERE

YOUR PRESENTS TO YOUR BABY

OTHER GIFTS RECEIVED / FROM WHOM

WHAT YOUR BABY ATE

SPECIAL MEMORIES

WHAT YOUR BABY WORE

FIRST BIRTHDAY

PLACE AND TIME

FOOD AND DRINK

THE CAKE

WHAT YOUR BABY WORE

OTHER CHILDREN PRESENT

ADULTS PRESENT

BIRTHDAY PHOTOGRAPH

GIFTS RECEIVED / FROM WHOM

MEMORABLE INCIDENTS

THE SECOND YEAR

Y OUR ONE YEAR OLD wants to explore everything within reach, and she tries to understand the world through these investigations. During her second year she will learn to walk, and will become increasingly mobile and independent. She will enjoy all kinds of physical games and activities, which will help her develop good muscle tone and fine-tune her skills. At this stage your child has very little memory or ability for premeditated thought. Because she has very little common sense and invariably tends to repeat mistakes, you or another adult need to keep an eye on her at all times. Your child needs to feel secure, and she relies upon her parents or other caregivers to act as her bedrock and interpreter of the world. Her ability to understand what people are saying will increase dramatically during this second year, although she will comprehend a great deal more than she is able to express verbally. At this time, she will also begin to imitate adults, copying things that she experiences or sees, and helping her parents as they go about their daily tasks. Your child also enjoys being with her peers, but does not, as yet, interact with them directly.

PHOTOGRAPH OF CHILD

MEMORABLE MILESTONES

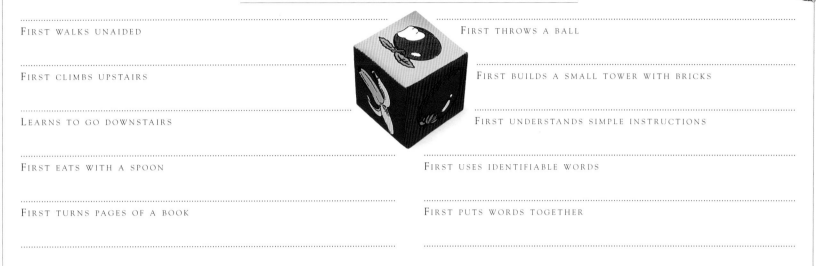

FIRST WALKS UNAIDED

FIRST CLIMBS UPSTAIRS

LEARNS TO GO DOWNSTAIRS

FIRST EATS WITH A SPOON

FIRST TURNS PAGES OF A BOOK

FIRST THROWS A BALL

FIRST BUILDS A SMALL TOWER WITH BRICKS

FIRST UNDERSTANDS SIMPLE INSTRUCTIONS

FIRST USES IDENTIFIABLE WORDS

FIRST PUTS WORDS TOGETHER

TREASURED MOMENTS

PERSONALITY

PHOTOGRAPH

YOUR CHILD'S VOCABULARY

MISPRONUNCIATIONS OF WORDS

WORDS FOR ANIMALS

WORDS FOR PEOPLE

THINGS THAT MAKE YOUR CHILD . . .

HAPPY OR AMUSED

EXCITED

HAVE A TANTRUM

FRIGHTENED OR NERVOUS

SPECIAL TRAITS

FAVORITE THINGS

FOOD

DRINK

TOYS AND GAMES

DOLL OR TEDDY

ANIMALS

SONGS AND RHYMES

BOOKS AND STORIES

CLOTHES

PHOTOGRAPH OF BEST FRIEND

FAVORITE ADULTS

SPECIAL FRIENDS

DAILY LIFE

DAILY ROUTINE

MORNING

MIDDAY

AFTERNOON

BATH TIME

BEDTIME

FAVORITE TIME OF DAY

WORST TIME OF DAY

SPECIAL MOMENTS

DESCRIPTION OF DAILY ACTIVITIES

PLAYING WITH FAVORITE TOYS

DRAWING AND PAINTING

LOOKING AT BOOKS

PUZZLES AND GAMES

PLAYING WITH DOUGH AND WATER

"HELPING" YOU

BATH TIME AND WATER PLAY

FAVORITE BATH TOYS

BATH TIME ACTIVITIES

PHOTOGRAPH OF BATH TIME

HOW YOUR CHILD PLAYS IN WATER

RESPONSE TO BEING BATHED

IN A KIDDIE POOL

RESPONSE TO HAIR BEING WASHED

IN A SWIMMING POOL

VACATIONS AND OUTINGS

ANNUAL VACATION

DATE

PLACE

THE TRIP

WHERE YOU STAYED

FAVORITE ACTIVITIES

NEW EXPERIENCES

SPECIAL MEMORIES

MEMORABLE OUTINGS

VISITS TO RELATIVES AND FRIENDS

OUTINGS TO THE COUNTRY/CITY

OTHER OUTINGS

VACATION PHOTOGRAPHS

HOLIDAYS AT TWO

WHERE HOLIDAY WAS SPENT

THE HOLIDAY MEAL

PHOTOGRAPH

WHO WAS THERE

OTHER GIFTS RECEIVED / FROM WHOM

WHAT YOUR CHILD WORE

YOUR PRESENTS TO YOUR CHILD

SPECIAL MEMORIES

SECOND BIRTHDAY

PLACE AND TIME

ENTERTAINMENT AND GAMES PLAYED

THE MOST POPULAR FOOD

THE CAKE

BIRTHDAY PHOTOGRAPH

OTHER CHILDREN PRESENT

GIFTS RECEIVED / FROM WHOM

ADULTS PRESENT

MEMORABLE INCIDENTS

THE THIRD YEAR

A TWO-YEAR-OLD CHILD has an insatiable curiosity about the world, and finds it endlessly fascinating. Your child will learn by assimilation and imitation, particularly through watching people going about their daily lives. Once he can talk he will ask questions constantly, and he will need to be introduced to new skills and activities so that he can broaden and enrich his experiences. Although the third year may sometimes be accompanied by tantrums, by the end of this year your child will become less self-centered. He will begin to be more accommodating toward others, and will make some attempt to develop the art of pleasing them. Physically, your child is becoming more competent and coordinated, and as his linguistic skills improve, so does his ability to express himself. At this stage of his development, your child views the world as a very physical place. He needs to be shown how to do things by being given practical demonstrations, rather than verbal explanations. At the beginning of this year, rather than play with other children directly, he will play alongside them in "parallel play," but as he reaches his third birthday, he will begin to enjoy the company of other children more and to participate in a variety of shared activities.

PHOTOGRAPH OF CHILD

MEMORABLE MILESTONES

FIRST DRINKS FROM A CUP WITHOUT A LID

FIRST SITS IN A NORMAL CHAIR

FIRST WASHES FACE

FIRST BRUSHES TEETH

FIRST GOES ALL DAY WITHOUT A DIAPER

FIRST TRIES TO GET DRESSED

FIRST SLEEPS IN A BED

FIRST RIDES A TRICYCLE

FIRST CATCHES A BALL

FIRST NAMES A COLOR

FIRST BEGINS TO COUNT

FIRST RECITES A NURSERY RHYME

TREASURED MOMENTS

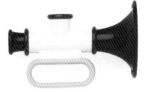

PERSONALITY

THINGS THAT MAKE YOUR CHILD . . .

HAPPY

....

AMUSED

....

EXCITED

....

HAVE A TANTRUM

....

FRIGHTENED OR NERVOUS

....

SPECIAL TRAITS

PHOTOGRAPH

YOUR CHILD'S VOCABULARY

MISPRONUNCIATIONS OF WORDS

....

WORDS FOR ANIMALS AND PEOPLE

FAVORITE THINGS

FOOD

DRINK

TOYS AND GAMES

PHOTOGRAPH OF
BEST FRIEND

DOLL OR TEDDY

ANIMALS

SONGS AND RHYMES

BOOKS AND STORIES

TELEVISION CHARACTERS

CLOTHES

FAVORITE ADULTS

SPECIAL FRIENDS

DAILY LIFE

DAILY ROUTINE

MORNING

MIDDAY

AFTERNOON

BATH TIME

BEDTIME

FAVORITE TIME OF DAY

WORST TIME OF DAY

DESCRIPTION OF DAILY ACTIVITIES

DRAWING AND PAINTING

MAKING THINGS

PLAYING WITH DOUGH AND CLAY

OUTDOOR GAMES

"HELPING" YOU

NURSERY SCHOOL

Name and address of nursery school
....
....

Date of first day
....

Names of teachers and helpers
....
....

Your feelings about the first day
....
....

Your child's reaction to the first day
....
....

Adjustment to nursery school
....
....

Your child's favorite activities
....
....

PHOTOGRAPH OF YOUR CHILD
GOING TO NURSERY SCHOOL

VACATIONS AND OUTINGS

ANNUAL VACATION

Date

Place

The trip

Where you stayed

Favorite activities

New experiences

Special memories

MEMORABLE OUTINGS

Visits to relatives and friends

Outings to the country/city

Other outings

VACATION PHOTOGRAPHS

HOLIDAYS AT THREE

WHERE HOLIDAY WAS SPENT

THE HOLIDAY MEAL

YOUR CHILD'S HAPPIEST MOMENTS

WHO WAS THERE

PHOTOGRAPH

YOUR PRESENTS TO YOUR CHILD

OTHER GIFTS RECEIVED / FROM WHOM

SPECIAL MEMORIES

THIRD BIRTHDAY

PLACE AND TIME

ENTERTAINMENT AND GAMES PLAYED

THE MOST POPULAR FOOD

BIRTHDAY PHOTOGRAPH

THE CAKE

OTHER CHILDREN PRESENT

ADULTS PRESENT

GIFTS RECEIVED / FROM WHOM

MEMORABLE INCIDENTS

THE FOURTH YEAR

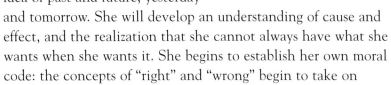

DURING HER FOURTH YEAR, your child begins to understand the concept of time and to grasp the idea of past and future, yesterday and tomorrow. She will develop an understanding of cause and effect, and the realization that she cannot always have what she wants when she wants it. She begins to establish her own moral code: the concepts of "right" and "wrong" begin to take on meaning and her consideration for others increases. She starts to offer instead of always taking, and she learns to befriend other children, share with them, take turns, and make compromises. As your child's skills develop, she is able to exert more control over her world, and she gains confidence in her abilities. Her manual dexterity increases and she is able to carry out a wide range of tasks. She will start to show an interest in writing and will concentrate for longer when listening to a story. By her fourth year, she will also be calmer and less prone to tantrums. Understanding everything she sees around her becomes very important, and she continues to act out real-life situations in imaginative play.

PHOTOGRAPH OF CHILD

MEMORABLE MILESTONES

FIRST EATS WITH A KNIFE AND FORK

FIRST DRAWS A RECOGNIZABLE FIGURE

FIRST COUNTS UP TO TWENTY AND FORMS LETTERS

FIRST COMPLETES A SIMPLE PUZZLE

FIRST DRESSES SELF PROPERLY

FIRST HOPS ON ONE FOOT

FIRST SKIPS

FIRST SHARES A TOY

TREASURED MOMENTS

PERSONALITY

PHOTOGRAPH

SPECIAL TRAITS

....

THINGS THAT MAKE YOUR CHILD . . .

HAPPY

LAUGH

EXCITED

CALM

THOUGHTFUL

ANGRY

INSECURE

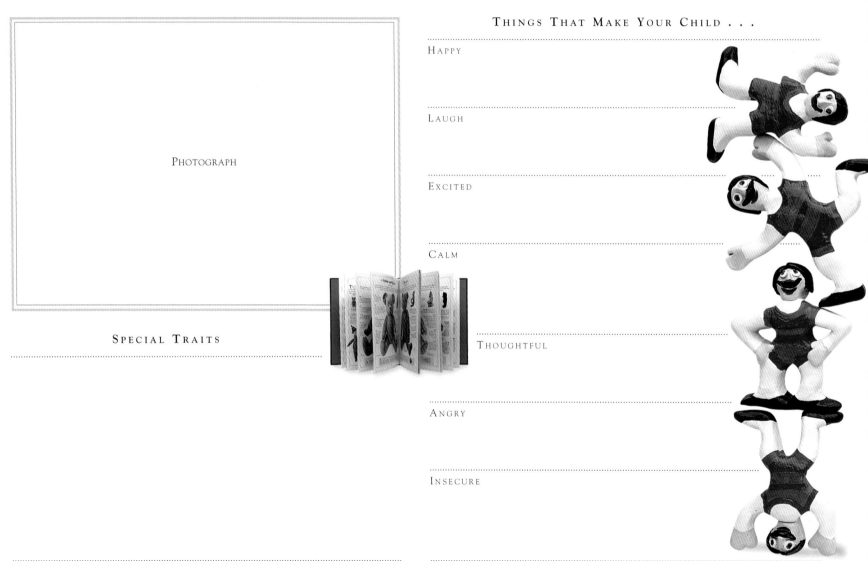

....

FAVORITE THINGS

FOOD

DRINK

TOYS

PHOTOGRAPH OF
BEST FRIEND

ANIMALS

SONGS AND RHYMES

SPORTS AND GAMES

BOOKS AND STORIES

TELEVISION CHARACTERS

CLOTHES

FAVORITE ADULTS

SPECIAL FRIENDS

DAILY LIFE

DAILY ROUTINE

MORNING

MIDDAY

AFTERNOON

BATH TIME

BEDTIME

WEEKLY ACTIVITIES

CLUBS AND CLASSES ATTENDED BY YOUR CHILD

DESCRIPTION OF DAILY ACTIVITIES

DRAWING AND PAINTING

MAKING THINGS

PLAYING WITH DOUGH AND CLAY

OUTDOOR GAMES

"HELPING" YOU

DRESSING UP

OTHER ACTIVITIES

VACATIONS AND OUTINGS

ANNUAL VACATION

DATE

PLACE

THE TRIP

WHERE YOU STAYED

FAVORITE ACTIVITIES

AMUSING INCIDENTS

SPECIAL MEMORIES

VACATION PHOTOGRAPH

MEMORABLE OUTINGS

VISITS TO RELATIVES AND FRIENDS

OTHER OUTINGS

HOLIDAYS AT FOUR

WHERE HOLIDAY WAS SPENT

THE HOLIDAY MEAL

YOUR CHILD'S HAPPIEST MOMENTS

PHOTOGRAPH

YOUR PRESENTS TO YOUR CHILD

OTHER GIFTS RECEIVED / FROM WHOM

WHO WAS THERE

SPECIAL MEMORIES

FOURTH BIRTHDAY

PLACE AND TIME

....

ENTERTAINMENT AND GAMES PLAYED

....

THE MOST POPULAR FOOD

....

THE CAKE

....

OTHER CHILDREN PRESENT

....

ADULTS PRESENT

....

BIRTHDAY PHOTOGRAPH

GIFTS RECEIVED / FROM WHOM

....

MEMORABLE INCIDENTS

....

THE FIFTH YEAR

BY THE FIFTH YEAR, your child is very able physically, and can run, jump, hop, skip, and climb with ease. Body and emotions remain closely related, and your child frequently articulates his feelings in a physical way – for example, he may jump in the air for joy or stamp his feet in anger. At this age a child likes the world to be well structured, and he may derive great satisfaction and enjoyment from categorizing and ordering things. Your child's vocabulary continues to expand, and with it the ability to express himself. He often asks pertinent and searching questions about the world around him, and he may wonder about other profound issues such as death and sex. Although your child's imagination continues to mature, he is very literal in his comprehension of things and remains highly impressionable. He becomes less dependent on his parents and relishes the company of other children. He enjoys playing with them and begins to form real friendships. This is the time when he starts to learn to exist in a wider world without his mother or father, and to enjoy the social experience of becoming part of a group.

PHOTOGRAPH OF CHILD

MEMORABLE MILESTONES

FIRST READS A WORD

FIRST RECITES OWN ADDRESS

FIRST WRITES OWN NAME

FIRST TELLS A JOKE

FIRST SWIMS UNAIDED

FIRST TIES OWN SHOELACES

FIRST RIDES A BICYCLE WITH TRAINING WHEELS

FIRST TELLS TIME

HANDWRITING SAMPLE

TREASURED MOMENTS

PERSONALITY

PHOTOGRAPH OR
HAND PRINT

SPECIAL TRAITS

························

THINGS THAT MAKE YOUR CHILD . . .

························

HAPPY

························

LAUGH

························

EXCITED

························

CALM

························

THOUGHTFUL

························

ANGRY

························

INSECURE

························

FAVORITE THINGS

FOOD

DRINK

TOYS

ANIMALS

SONGS AND RHYMES

SPORTS AND GAMES

PHOTOGRAPH OF
BEST FRIEND

BOOKS AND STORIES

TELEVISION CHARACTERS

CLOTHES

FAVORITE ADULTS

SPECIAL FRIENDS

DAILY LIFE

DAILY ROUTINE

MORNING

MIDDAY

AFTERNOON

BATH TIME

BEDTIME

WEEKLY ACTIVITIES

CLUBS AND CLASSES ATTENDED BY YOUR CHILD

DESCRIPTION OF DAILY ACTIVITIES

DRAWING AND PAINTING

MAKING THINGS

PLAYING WITH DOUGH AND CLAY

OUTDOOR GAMES

"HELPING" YOU

DRESSING UP

OTHER ACTIVITIES

FIRST DAYS AT SCHOOL

NAME AND ADDRESS OF SCHOOL

DATE OF FIRST DAY

NAME OF TEACHER

NAME OF PRINCIPAL

SCHEDULE OF SCHOOL DAY

YOUR FEELINGS ABOUT THE FIRST DAY

YOUR CHILD'S COMMENTS ON THE DAY

PHOTOGRAPH OF YOUR CHILD
GOING TO SCHOOL

FAVORITE CLASSROOM ACTIVITIES

NAMES OF OTHER CHILDREN

VACATIONS AND OUTINGS

ANNUAL VACATION

DATE

PLACE

THE TRIP

WHERE YOU STAYED

FAVORITE ACTIVITIES

AMUSING INCIDENTS

SPECIAL MEMORIES

MEMORABLE OUTINGS

VISITS TO RELATIVES AND FRIENDS

OUTINGS TO THE COUNTRY/CITY

OTHER OUTINGS

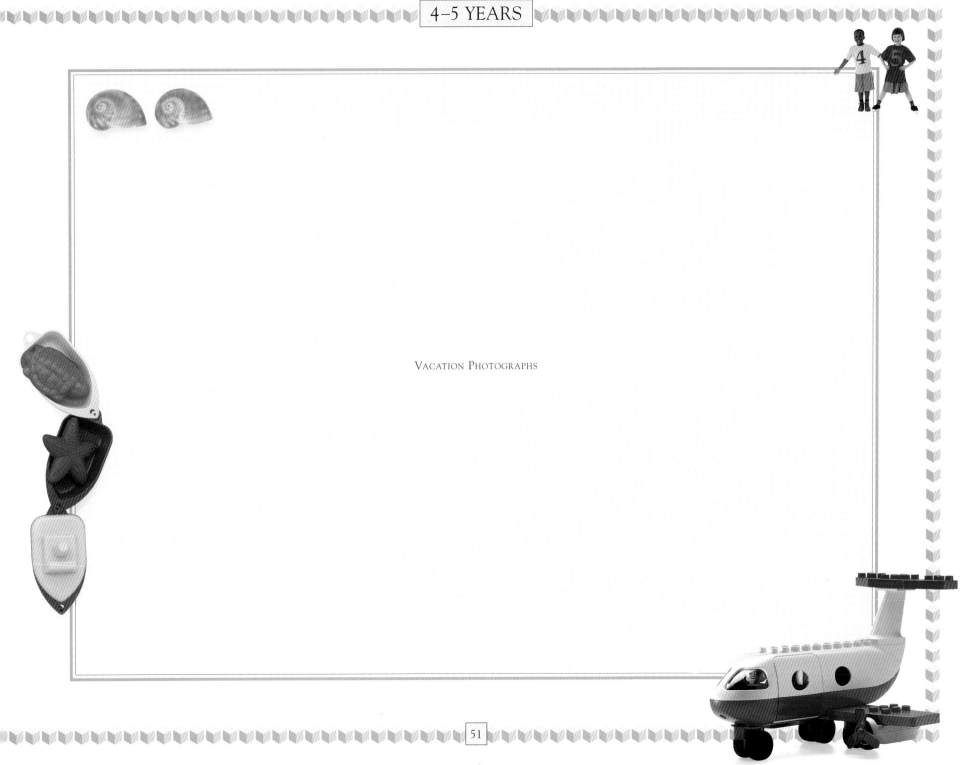

Vacation Photographs

HOLIDAYS AT FIVE

WHERE HOLIDAY WAS SPENT

THE HOLIDAY MEAL

YOUR CHILD'S HAPPIEST MOMENTS

WHO WAS THERE

YOUR PRESENTS TO YOUR CHILD

PHOTOGRAPH

OTHER GIFTS RECEIVED / FROM WHOM

SPECIAL MEMORIES

FIFTH BIRTHDAY

PLACE AND TIME

ENTERTAINMENT AND GAMES PLAYED

THE MOST POPULAR FOOD

THE CAKE

OTHER CHILDREN PRESENT

BIRTHDAY PHOTOGRAPH

ADULTS PRESENT

GIFTS RECEIVED / FROM WHOM

MEMORABLE INCIDENTS

GROWTH RECORD

AGE	HEIGHT	WEIGHT	CLOTHING SIZE	SHOE SIZE
SIX MONTHS				
ONE YEAR				
EIGHTEEN MONTHS				
TWO YEARS				
TWO AND A HALF YEARS				
THREE YEARS				
THREE AND A HALF YEARS				
FOUR YEARS				
FOUR AND A HALF YEARS				
FIVE YEARS				
NOTES				

Mark your child's height and weight on these graphs at six-month intervals. Use imperial or metric measurements, but do not mix them.

Height

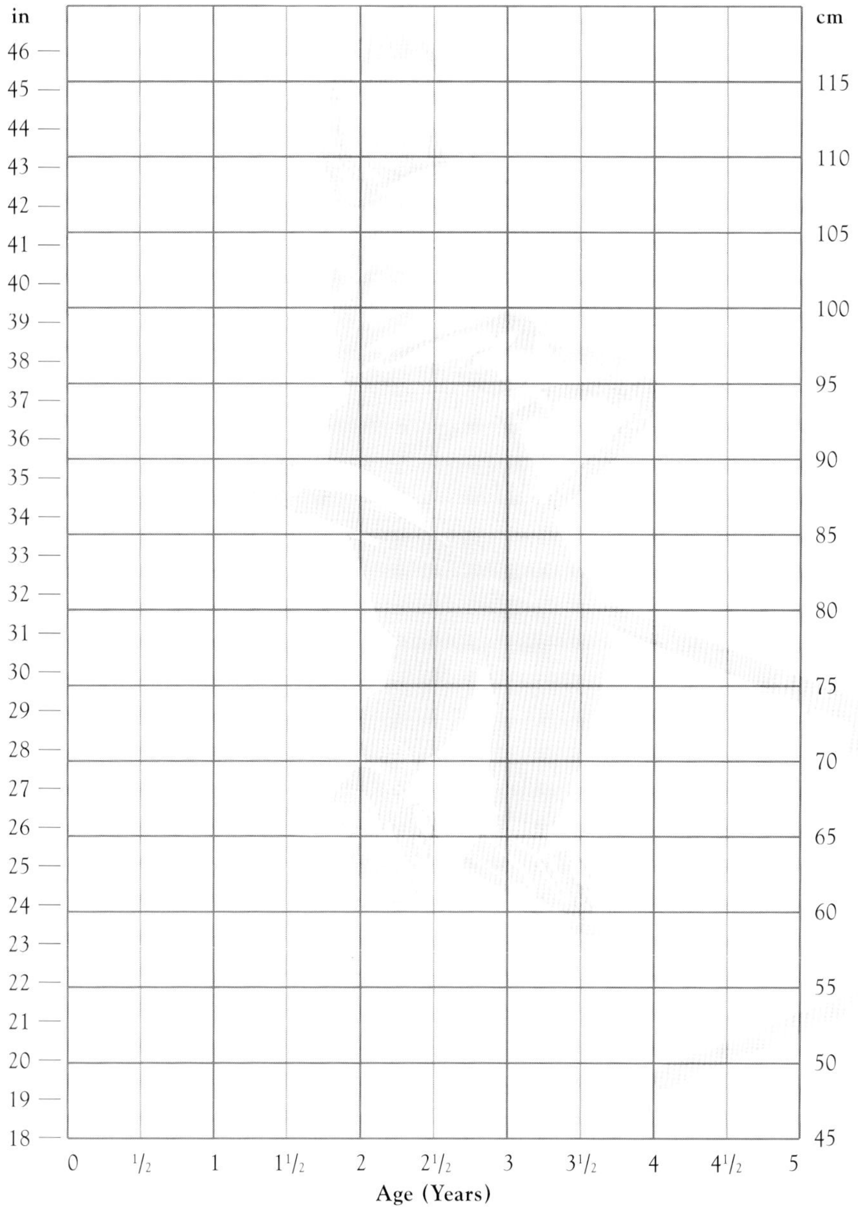
in
46
45
44
43
42
41
40
39
38
37
36
35
34
33
32
31
30
29
28
27
26
25
24
23
22
21
20
19
18
cm
115
110
105
100
95
90
85
80
75
70
65
60
55
50
45
0 1/2 1 1 1/2 2 2 1/2 3 3 1/2 4 4 1/2 5
Age (Years)

Weight

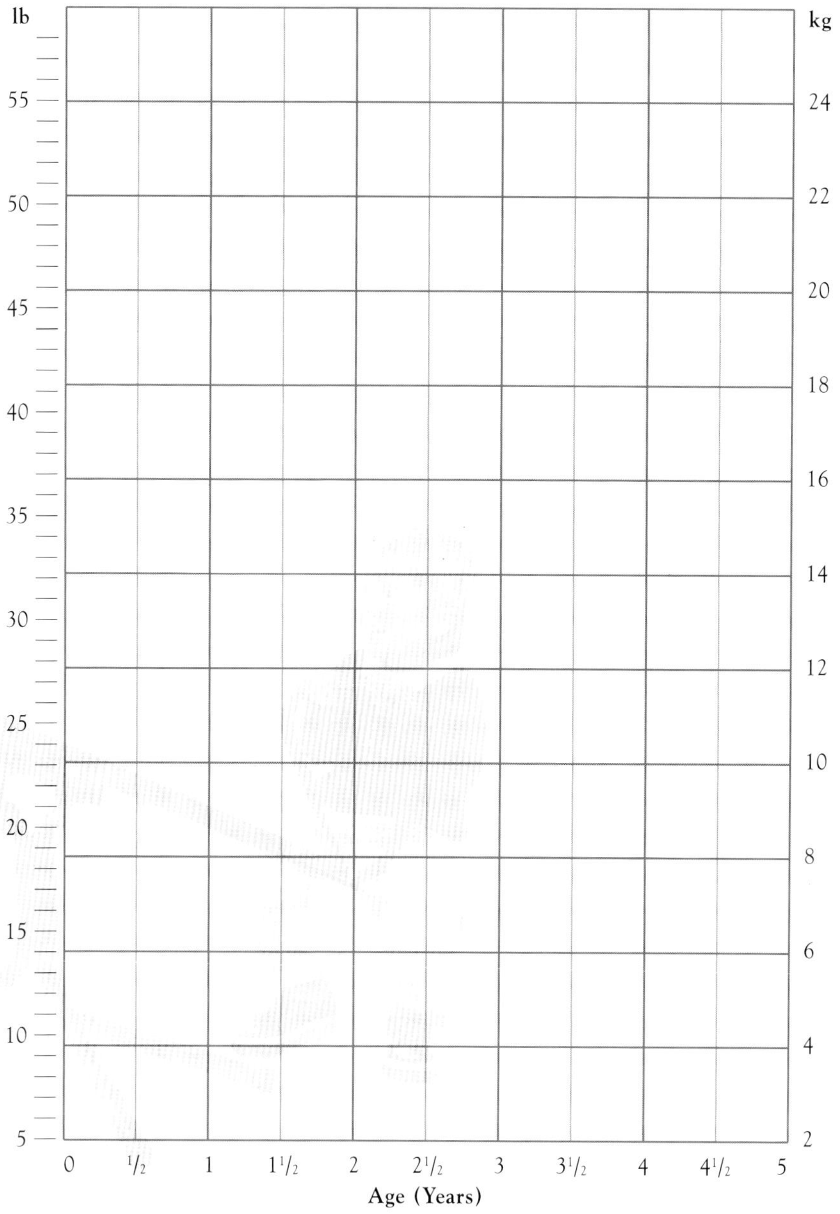
lb
55
50
45
40
35
30
25
20
15
10
5
kg
24
22
20
18
16
14
12
10
8
6
4
2
0 1/2 1 1 1/2 2 2 1/2 3 3 1/2 4 4 1/2 5
Age (Years)

MEDICAL RECORD

TEETHING

	Age	Date
FIRST TOOTH		
SECOND TOOTH		
THIRD TOOTH		
FOURTH TOOTH		
FIFTH TOOTH		
SIXTH TOOTH		
SEVENTH TOOTH		
EIGHTH TOOTH		
NINTH TOOTH		
TENTH TOOTH		

IMMUNIZATIONS

Vaccine	Age	Date
DIPHTHERIA/TETANUS/ WHOOPING COUGH (DTP)		
POLIO (IPV) (OPV)		
MENINGITIS (HIB)		
MEASLES/MUMPS/ RUBELLA (MMR)		
OTHER VACCINES		

TESTS

Test	Age	Date
HEARING		
EYE		
GENERAL MEDICAL		

CHILDHOOD ILLNESSES

Diagnosis	Age	Date

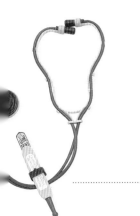